THE POWER OF POETRY

Share Your Voice

Edited By Wendy Laws

First published in Great Britain in 2023 by:

Young Writers
Remus House
Coltsfoot Drive
Peterborough
PE2 9BF
Telephone: 01733 890066
Website: www.youngwriters.co.uk

Book Design by Ashley Janson

Softback ISBN 978-1-80459-577-0

Printed and bound in the UK by BookPrintingUK
Website: www.bookprintinguk.com
YB0542QZ

DESTRUCTION DISASTER WAR POVERTY EQUALITY THE FUTURE HOPE

FOREWORD

Since 1991, here at Young Writers we have celebrated the awesome power of creative writing, especially in young adults where it can serve as a vital method of expressing their emotions and views about the world around them. In every poem we see the effort and thought that each student published in this book has put into their work and by creating this anthology we hope to encourage them further with the ultimate goal of sparking a life-long love of writing.

Our latest competition for secondary school students, **The Power of Poetry,** challenged young writers to consider what was important to them and how to express that using the power of words. We wanted to give them a voice, the chance to express themselves freely and honestly, something which is so important for these young adults to feel confident and listened to. They could give an opinion, highlight an issue, consider a dilemma, impart advice or simply write about something they love. There were no restrictions on style or subject so you will find an anthology brimming with a variety of poetic styles and topics. We hope you find it as absorbing as we have.

We encourage young writers to express themselves and address subjects that matter to them, which sometimes means writing about sensitive or contentious topics. If you have been affected by any issues raised in this book, details on where to find help can be found at
www.youngwriters.co.uk/info/other/contact-lines

DISCRIMINATION BULLYING POLLUTION IDENTITY POWER DREAMS

CONTENTS

THE POEMS

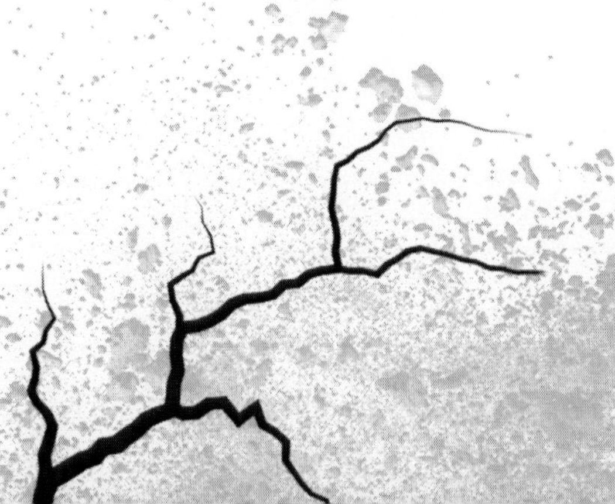

PTSD

The days were cold, stars bring dim light.
A bang in the distance, I take off to the right.
Another bang to my back, sounds piercing my ears.
I crawl on the ground, face covered in tears.

The shops disappear, replaced by trenches.
Curl up on the ground, left there defenceless.
Another bang echoes, I ask when the end is.
Spiralling down, I'm losing my senses.

I look to the sky, thinking my last breath's been drawn.
I see colours fly, red, green and blue.
Orange and pink, flames shaped like stars.
They're just fireworks, so high, so far.

I climb off the ground, to my house I tread.
Not scared anymore, still, off I sped.
Those bangs from the sky still ring in my head.
Tomorrow I dread, those memories haunt me again.

Orestes-Owen Njogu-Vrakas (14)
Bishop Challoner Catholic College, Birmingham

Rain

Every day it's raining,
Every day my home is changing.
I've got nothing to lose,
My fate isn't mine to choose.
I'm a refugee of Ukraine; the land of the landmines.
The country forgotten by The Times.
More people care about Kanye's marriage
And they've forgotten the constant barrage.
Our constant fight for survival,
I'm begging for my father's revival.
Wish that magic was real,
Wish we could use it to heal.
Hoping that this world stops bleeding,
Hoping that I don't stop breathing,
Hope my mates will stop leaving,
Hope their mothers will stop grieving,
Hope is a funny little thing,
We rely on it, like a couple with a ring
And now I'm clinging onto my home.
When I knock on the door, would Solomiya be home
Or will I be there on my own, all alone?
I pray for an end to Putin,
They know I'll be in Moscow shootin'
Bullets straight to his cranium,
I know that man's not titanium.

Damned if I do, damned if I don't,
With everyone singing my praises like Robert de Niro,
But without anyone to celebrate with, I'd be nothing,
I'd be zero
And if I don't do it
The rain will never end
And I'll drown in the deep end.

George Jones (15)
Bishop Challoner Catholic College, Birmingham

Social Anxiety

I lay here as I obey the tiredness.
Sleep consumes me as my dream begins to bloom.
My eyes twitch as I switch sides on my pillow.
I get up from the extreme dream that floods my mind.
I continue my day whilst I wonder what to say.
It's not easy having social anxiety.
Not being able to reconnect perfectly like everyone.
I waste the day away not being able to say,
"Hey, how are you today?"
My mind continues to race as time goes by at a fast pace.
There she is right in front of me.
My eyes ponder as I wonder and ponder.
My mouth is stuck. Not again,
Just then her hair catches my eye, that perfect hair.
I felt so bad, I looked without a care.
The day continues as if it's new.
After I step into the blue,
I threw my bag like a rag on the floor.
I then shut my door as I pour my heart out,
I begin to shout, "How could I allow myself such disgrace
With this race being run?"
It's her last year here.
I need to get it off my chest so I can finally rest.

Hopefully, I'll make it and not break it.
Let's see hopefully.
Now I must go and rest so I can try my best.

Rex Healy (14)
Bishop Challoner Catholic College, Birmingham

Tsunami

I came from the earthquake under the sea,
Crumbling and rumbling waiting to be free,
Pushing up with all my force,
An explosion even bigger than a golf course.

Swallowing the ocean in one big mouthful,
Releasing a wave as tall as a swimming pool,
Sending it out onto the shore,
The fastest wave ever before.

When it reached the city with a mighty crash,
The land is destroyed with one big splash,
Devouring the country in one weighty swig,
All that is left is one feeble twig.

Bodies slumped over trees,
Like a deadly, toxic, fatal disease,
Swept into the wave goes houses and land,
Hurling across to the next beach of sand.

Demolishing ships and small fishing boats,
Moving on fast, aiming for the throat,
Cutting and slicing and mashing and bashing,
Making people die in the water thrashing.

I then moved on to the next city in sight,
Circling out and increasing in height,

Slamming to the next land visible,
Laughing inside, I am invincible.

Squashing the buildings one by one,
Wait one or two seconds and then they are gone,
Destroyed forever, land slumps underwater,
I am the big, giant, backstabbing squatter.

I am the one responsible for millions of deaths,
Worldwide, every year I swallow people's last breaths,
I'm just one wave that sits on the sea,
But I'm different to usual, I'm a lethal, toxic, explosive tsunami.

Daphne Brett (12)
Broughton High School, Edinburgh

Decapitation

Do you ever hear a cackling sound
that makes you fear to turn around?
Sometimes when you're all alone
you wonder if you're not quite on your own.
Maybe you see in the corner of your eye
a glimpse of me just passing by.
Most people fail to notice the knife
that might just come to end your life.

It isn't your imagination
when I commit your decapitation.
Slowly cutting through the skin
the knife keeps going in and in.
As your heart rate starts to drop
all of a sudden, it abruptly stops.
The blade has finally made it through
guess what? Now it's over for you.

To Edinburgh morgue your body goes
just so it doesn't decompose.
By the way, I still have your head
and yet another knife that's been stained red.
I've climbed Arthur's Seat all the way to the top
and brought the head to watch it drop.
There it goes rolling down
all the way back into town.

I made my way back to the bottom
I could just leave the head to go rotten.
The police have arrived, I guess they've been told
the look on their faces never gets old.
The head will be buried along with the body
the coffin will probably be very bloody.
Now I've told you how it was done
but it's not over yet, there will be more fun...

Cleopatra Ross (12)
Broughton High School, Edinburgh

Friends Like You And Me

Friends change
from time to time
and no, this isn't all going to rhyme.
Friends change
as seasons come and go
but I know we will grow
even when the leaves
grow and grow.

Friends can be weird
their personality can change
or just in general
but I know
you aren't like that
you stay by my side.
Unlike the others
we glide through life together
I've never met anyone like you.
My trust will live
for as long as the sky is blue.

Maybe I did rhyme.
It doesn't matter
because I love you.

Honor Llewellin (12)
Broughton High School, Edinburgh

Friendship

If I fall
will you stay for it all?
When things get rough
will you help me stay tough?
Friendships are hard.
Am I easy for you to discard?
Whispering scenes,
what do they mean?
Friendships are hard
but when you play the right cards
they will come along
singing your song.
Even on the darkest day
they make your smile sneak out some way,
so hold close the ones there no matter what,
friendships are hard
but together or apart
true friends hold a special place in my heart.

Bibi Coane (12)
Broughton High School, Edinburgh

Boys' Stereotype

I am the one you think sits in the corner throwing pieces of paper at you.
I am the one you think of when you see a gang.
I am the one that you think will hurt you and laugh behind your back.
I am the one you think won't care about the future
But you're wrong...
Not all boys are like that.
Some are...
Kind
Trustworthy
Friendly
Nice
Funny
And respectful
So when you see a boy or boys...
Just think first.

Dexter Holmes (12)
Broughton High School, Edinburgh

Stuck In A Loop!

Have you ever noticed yourself doing the same thing every single day?
What you eat, drink or to what you wear,
Most of the time, it can be a bit boring.
For example, my life.
All I do is wake up, get dressed, eat, then go to school,
Then after learning, I go home, eat dinner, watch TV then sleep.
Then in the morning, I wake up and do it all over again.
I am stuck in a loop!

Moksha Melam (12)
Broughton High School, Edinburgh

The Love Loop

I feel like I'm going to be
stuck in this
endless loop
of loving you
to not loving you,
then loving you again.
Though you may not love me
you somehow found the key,
the key to unlock me
from this loop,
but you won't
set me free.

Poppy Raw (12)
Broughton High School, Edinburgh

The Future

F ossil fuels are killing our forests
U nless we change, I will not rest
T he time is now, to do our best
U nless we change, we can say goodbye
R ising temperatures fill the sky
E veryone listen, the future is up to you and me.

Sophie Russell (12)
Broughton High School, Edinburgh

The Beautiful Game

Football, otherwise known as the beautiful game,
Has been flowing through my body since birth, with many aspects of the beautiful game,

Blood that gives me love to play and watch the beautiful game,
Passion that allows me to persevere when times get hard in the beautiful game,
Strength that flows through my limbs to not fall when I tire in the beautiful game.

Love that creates support for teams in the beautiful game,
Hate for other teams that defeat my team in the beautiful game,
Addiction for watching the many leagues and cups across the globe in the beautiful game.

Togetherness to link with other supporters of club and country in the beautiful game,
Rivalries to link with supporters of other clubs and countries for bittersweet aftermath in the beautiful game.
Relief for when my team flies to the top in the beautiful game,
Regret when my team fails to reach the top in the beautiful game.

Nostalgia to remember all those who came before and succeeded in the beautiful game,
Modernness to reflect on the young of today to see how high they can go in the beautiful game.

Controversy to debate on thoughts of today and before in the beautiful game,
Agreement to bring ideas on factual information to our thoughts in the beautiful game.

Resentment to those who think it is okay to discriminate against players in the beautiful game,
Adoration for those who oppose and right those discriminators in the beautiful game.

Football doesn't just create a few feelings of happiness or sadness,
It instead creates many aspects of love, passion and hate for the beautiful game.

Vihaan Sule (14)
Colchester Royal Grammar School, Colchester

World Problems

W orld problems are things that halt society from developing
O verpopulation causes deforestation for more homes to be built
R ainforests are being destroyed, the Amazon rainforest has lost 13.2% itself due to deforestation
L arge amounts of unemployment occur causing lots of families to go into poverty
D etaching large amounts of plastic from the oceans can help stop marine life from dying.

P ollution fills the air, land and sea and it increases the risk of heart disease and lung cancer in humans
R ainforests give us 28% of our oxygen but we carry on cutting the rainforests down
O pen yourself up and try to help the living things around you
B egin to try to make a difference
L eaving everything as it is and not doing anything will only cause larger problems
E xtinction of many animals is caused by hunters
M arine plants give us 70% of our oxygen but we are repaying marine plants by polluting the ocean
S o we need to help each other to resolve these world problems.

Gabriel Ivanov (14)
Colchester Royal Grammar School, Colchester

Mixed Cultures

I was born as a child of an immigrant family
who travelled on a journey to the West.
I was born and raised under the English nationality,
immersed and surrounded by Western culture,
grown to enjoy food, cinema and music naturally.

However, I grew following and interested in my family's culture,
admiring the traditions, stories and cuisine.
I grew to speak a broken native language,
but an understanding of the speech of those who speak it.
An incomplete capability to communicate with my family.

I am partially disconnected from my relatives
and some being exceptionally distant,
but I still find solutions, that have to be creative.
To patch up the holes in my connections
and learn more about our traditions

I learnt to be prepared,
to compensate for what's missing.
I was born in unique mixed cultures
that I learnt to be proud to be a part of.

Lucas Wong (14)
Colchester Royal Grammar School, Colchester

The Influence Of Getting Older

I sit here as a once oblivious youth
I dream about my future
I dream about life after death
I dream about the truth.

We need to ignore the stereotypes
We let them define us
We grow older with a preset view
We are taken over by media types.

I think about my limits and they don't seem that much
I think about my future
I think about when they will be lower
I think about when they'll be out of touch.

We need to see the mental damage we've caused
We will defy the rules
We will break limits
We won't let age limits become our laws.

I know that age won't tell me what to do
I know I will be stronger
I know I will be alive for infinity
I know stereotypes are fake and not true.

We will live forever in this world of lies
We won't let it overrule us
You are perfect no matter what age
You are the master of your own destiny.

Hudson Williams (13)

Colchester Royal Grammar School, Colchester

The Forgotten Poppy

I am a little poppy,
As bright as bright can be,
But I'm definitely not perfect,
As you will see in the story of me.

It all started when I sprouted,
My little, little leaf,
I poked up my little eye to see,
But I saw nothing but grief.

Guns and bombs at an instance,
I was scared and alone,
Nowhere to call home,
But then I found it: somewhere to call my own.

A soldier put his gun down,
To pick my body up,
But as he was going to run to the trench,
I fell and landed in a shrub.

When I turned around,
I was heartbroken to see,
The horror of the soldier
And it was there I began my plea.

So here I stand,
In the army of poppies,

Looking over the land,
Thinking about it every day.

I am a little poppy,
As bright as bright can be,
But I'm definitely not perfect,
As you have seen in the story of me.

Finn Poole-O'Hara (12)
Colchester Royal Grammar School, Colchester

The Power Of Words

Ever since the beginning; the dawn of mankind,
Words have been the most powerful force of mind,
Words can be spoken, whispered, written, remembered, forgotten,
Words have the power to heal, harm, humiliate, humble,
Think about the power we wield.

Words can be a beacon of inspiration,
Words can grant you liberation,
Words can motivate and push you to great heights,
Words can separate wrongs from rights.

Words can divide us into factions,
Words can destroy nations,
Words can be used for miscreants,
Words can be engraved in permanence.

History can change with just a clause,
Just a word flowed can change your cause,
We must take great caution when words are said,
For there are no U-turns when they are read,
Words from a mouth are like arrows shot from a bow,
Both cannot be returned once they are let go.

Zaim Ali (12)
Colchester Royal Grammar School, Colchester

The Earth

At the beginning of time, everything was dark and dull.
There was no life,
No happiness and I was lonely.
When I found them I saw potential,
The potential for good.

I protected and shielded them from the darkness of space.
I looked after them and nurtured them for all their lives.
I gave all I had to make them happy.
I tried to make them content thinking they would be kind in return.

Instead of the love I expected all I got was hatred.
They pumped smoke into my air,
Poisoned my waters
And stole precious materials from my belly.

Finally I had had enough,
I sent down whirling tornadoes to tear up the ground,
Searing lava from my insides
And acidic rain from the clouds.
I made sure I brought ruin to all of them.

It was foolish to trust those beings,
But now I am back to where I was before.

Daniel Chennattu (12)
Colchester Royal Grammar School, Colchester

Our Wonderful World

How happy are those once pink pigs now they're rotting in the mud?
Maybe just pink isn't their thing
as they are staring up in the mud, carrots, celery and spuds.
All that is foolish is not elephants, by all accounts is wise, now knowing this is a fact as they know how the elephant can surprise.
Zebras have stripes and can gallop away, while monkeys in the tree do sway.
Old crocodile swims in the pool so deep or lies out in the sun to sleep.
The birds fly high in the sky all day, go over hills and far away but when night falls and it begins to rain, they all go hide in their little caves.
The tiger in the jungle hides and he blinks his big orange eyes.
He sneaks between the trees to find some dinner and some peace of mind.
That is our wonderful world and this is how it should stay and you can help today and make this world a better place.

Hayden Lynn (12)
Colchester Royal Grammar School, Colchester

The Earth's Lament

Cliffs of ice thunder into the sea,
As the sea boils angrily and the cracked wind cries,
"How can this be? How can this be?"

Sparks erupt, fireballs of a Roman candle,
Amongst dying trees,
Acrid ash, embers smoulder -
A burning issue for generations.

Rivers lie lifeless like fallow fields in winter,
A bounty of desiccated fish strewn in clouds of dust.

Waves advance, an onrushing army on crumbling shores.
Intense precipitation precipitates the suffering;
The rain surrenders, the suffering endures.

Inexorable harm is inflicted on humanity's home,
Life's safe repository vanishing
Like a mist of breath on a mirror.
Standing on the brink of an unknown future,
The Earth's soul sighs, "How can this be? How can this be?"

Valentino Calleja (12)
Colchester Royal Grammar School, Colchester

A Feeling Of Happiness

'B out time you acknowledge your surrounding
U nder the glistening sun
T ogether with no friends frowning

Y ou wish, that is how your life is done
O xillating energy surrounds you
U ltimate calmness you feel

A fter looking at all the blue
R ivers flowing beneath the heel
E verything can't go any better

D reams aren't as perfect as this
E xuberation that can't be put in a letter
P erfect life with bliss
R emembrance comes back to you
E verything suddenly fades
S uddenly everything comes back to you
S adness joins the shades
E verything was just a dream
D epressed you are and always will be.

Ibrahim Mohamed (13)
Colchester Royal Grammar School, Colchester

Sky

Shades of blue, pink, yellow and white
And even black in the dead of night.
Millions of colours in that huge sky,
Where joyful birds come to fly.

When the sky is blue, the sun comes to play,
It stays there playing until the end of the day.
When the moon takes its place and holds on tight,
Then stays there until the end of the night.

But sometimes the moon tries to overstay its welcome
And hide in the mellow blue.
But the sun rises up with a swirl of colours,
Turning clouds into candyfloss and changing blue to red too.

The sky will always be there: in the cold or the warm,
It will even stay strong in a dreary storm.
I know that after the lightning and rain,
The birds will fly joyfully once again.

Barnaby Alexander (11)
Colchester Royal Grammar School, Colchester

Wednesday's The Greatest Day

Her raven black hair and her fierce daring eyes
Her colossal courage such that it matters not her size
When fear sees her it dashes away
The name of my inspiration is Wednesday.

Her features and skin so impossibly bleak
Yet she has such an incredible physique
The creatures and critters, she sees us as weak
No doubt Wednesday's the best day of the week.

Her inspiration runs deep through my core
It's Wednesday Addams who I adore
This infatuation with her is definitely unhealthy
Wednesday Addams is nothing short of wealthy.

Her abilities are definitely extraordinary
Nothing of Wednesday Addams is ordinary
Her utilities though used are not needed
Wednesday Addams is a name to be heeded.

Michael Duran (13)
Colchester Royal Grammar School, Colchester

My Friend's Journey

Together we welcome a brand new day,
I am the wiry, verdant grass,
you are the lapis sky with crispy clouds,
this new spring morning is a wonderful dance.

And the happiness I bring you is all that you desire,
the flower, the bliss, the sunshine and the breeze,
and all of our friendship and elation we share,
would be proven by the merry, buzzing bees.

And with the season's end, our friendship grows,
the summer breeze brings warmth and happiness as
I play to you with tuneful xylophones,
you sing me a song of innocence.

Sometimes the autumn tinges our friendship
or frosty disagreements take hold,
but every year, I know we'll start a new journey
with spring our fellowship becomes bold.

Kingsley He (12)
Colchester Royal Grammar School, Colchester

Future Planet

All around us, nature has disappeared,
Precious ice caps and glaciers destroyed,
Fierce forest infernos rapidly spread,
They won't save the future of our planet.

Leaders say they'll cut back on fossil fuels,
But they don't understand the urgency,
As they pump out harmful false promises,
They could save the future of our planet.

Protect our air and seas begging for care,
Be kind to the Earth, there's not another,
Tomorrow is being stolen from us,
We must save the future of our planet.

Now stand up and fight in our climate war,
Small actions from all, soldiers to battle,
For the sake of coming generations,
You must save the future of our planet.

Samuel Park (14)
Colchester Royal Grammar School, Colchester

The Game Of The World

I don't know what makes me who I am
It could be my beliefs or it could be I'm a man.
Maybe it's not those at all
It could be the game I've played since I was small.
The game I've loved since I could crawl
The game of the world... football.
It's a game of the mind but the game of our hearts
When football is played it's like flawless art.
A game which can make you soar
But could also feel like a savage war.
A game to support your family, your country, your city
But can fill your soul with so much pity.
If your club wins you're happy as can be,
But if they lose they feel shackled and away from the free.
Yet I don't know, maybe football is what made me.

Sami Martin (13)
Colchester Royal Grammar School, Colchester

This World Is Our Duty

Oh what a piteous spectacle our Earth must look to a foreign planet,
looking down on our squabbles and wants and desires,
turning our environment into a quagmire.

How we mine coal and metal,
yet not care for the flower's petal?

Trees' mighty trunks are felled down to the earth,
their once healthy soil now a fiery hearth.

Over the world coral reefs die,
whilst jet planes streak smoke across the blue sky.

We played a gamble, rolled the dice
and who's to pay? Why the bears on the ice!

This world is our own, this world is our home,
yet why can't we leave this world alone?
It is our duty, it is our pride, so let's make this issue subside!

Leo Hart (12)
Colchester Royal Grammar School, Colchester

The Wind

Slowly, softly, the wind blows,
Rustling through the grass
Like a tidal wave of green.

A solitary man stands at a bus stop,
The rain pouring on him.
The wind flurries around,
Shielding him from the rain.
A lone bird flies up in the clouds,
Struggling to keep up with its flock.
The wind tickles its feathers,
Spurring it onwards.
A sole child sits on a bench,
Weeping inconsolably.
The wind envelops her,
Whispering in her ear, bringing comfort.
Two smiling people are getting married,
Fragrant blossoms falling on them.
The wind brushes past them,
Ruffling their hair in joy.

Wherever you are, whatever you do,
A wind will be there for you.

Jakov Radunović (11)
Colchester Royal Grammar School, Colchester

Hoop Dreams

Hi basketball, it's me
another one of the kids you inspired
to be the best they can be
and to ignite the fire.

Since I was a boy
I've wanted to play
so my dad bought a toy
and day after day

I got better and better.
No matter the weather
I would train and train
even play through the pain.

I wasn't going to stop
I was climbing to the top
I was dribbling the ball
but I wasn't growing tall.

You gave me this dream
and I will achieve it.
It might sound obscene
but I believe it.

Hi basketball, it's me
another one of the kids you inspired
to be the best they can be
and to ignite the fire.

Miguel Kitasoboka (12)
Colchester Royal Grammar School, Colchester

Love Ukraine

L et us reward their utmost bravery, support Ukraine,
O n the ground, patriots fight fiercely, support Ukraine,
V ictory awaits the army to gain, support Ukraine,
E very Ukrainian anxious from the pain, support Ukraine.

U nder shelters, people cry in the cold, support Ukraine,
K ids, so young, fleeing homes as told, support Ukraine,
R ifles, guns and tanks reign the land, support Ukraine,
A nger and danger have made love so bland, support Ukraine,
I n times so tough, citizens come together, support Ukraine,
N o pain this quick stabs light as a feather, support Ukraine,
E nemies with ego come together forever, love Ukraine.

Krish Sutharsan (12)
Colchester Royal Grammar School, Colchester

Mystery

Mystery,
It's like an endless void of questions,
The shadows rage like an inferno in your mind.
Never letting you rest, never letting you think.
The only thought is an answer to your question.
The question that no one but you knows.
It's the burden that you carry till you find the answer.
Until you find it, something in you will always be missing.
The creature that always pesters you,
And over time it slowly becomes a monster.
Until...
The light that you've sought after penetrates it.
It overcomes the troubles and the pure black flames of sadness.
It destroys every malicious thought.
It gives you hope as realisation kicks in.
You have found an answer.

Adheesh Rajasekaran (11)
Colchester Royal Grammar School, Colchester

My Two Fumes

I have two fumes and they've mixed, they've flown and
they've grown.
Whereof they've both tuned, hereof they've remixed, they've
blown and yes they're not a clone.
One fume is strong in the kitchen, yet sleeping in politics can
be wrong but rich in the kitchen, yet it has an obsession with
recession.

My two fumes have names, one fume is called Nigeria, the
other, England.
Hmm, are they lame?
There's one moon, yet they're unmixed, they're torn, alone
but one fume is where fun can gloom, some particles go on
planes, a new society born?
The other fume tears into countries and cities, some awake,
ditches the poor yet have an obsession for progression.

Damilola Odetola (14)
Colchester Royal Grammar School, Colchester

Birds

Let's go explore the great outdoors,
In the forest there are parrots and macaws,
Robins are something we can adore,
But let's head to the park because there's still more.

Swans swimming in the sea,
Blackbirds walking across the street,
Pigeons soaring in the breeze
And a magpie trying to steal my keys.

Owls hooting in the night
And peacocks' feathers - a beautiful sight!
Seeing bluetits gives me delight
And it's cool to see crows taking flight.

Birds are everywhere all around,
You can see them without a sound,
Take pictures of them when they're around
And there are other birds waiting to be found.

Tahmeed Rahman (11)
Colchester Royal Grammar School, Colchester

Lockdown

L ying on the sofa all alone
O nline gaming whilst my parents are not home.
C hecking the time, wondering when they are coming back,
K illing the time in any way possible.
D oodling in my notebook, waiting for class to end,
O ffering my friends to play,
W inning games but they don't stay,
N ever leaving the house, due to lockdown.

I magining what it would be like outside,
S ighing as I think how life is upside down.

B ored all day with nothing to do.
A ngry with teachers during online school.
D ying to go outside, but waiting for the lockdown to end.

Arian Hossain (12)
Colchester Royal Grammar School, Colchester

A Picture In The Air

Day by day I see some change
in this lovely planet of ours.
I make a picture in the air,
a picture that will shortly never be made.

I see a flower of straw,
just hoping it doesn't roar.
It is hiding in the grass,
staring at its target and ready to advance.

Around him is a wonderful scene,
I just can't believe this isn't a dream.
The petals of magical mountains, the turns of the rivers,
can you not see why you shouldn't reconsider?

Day by day I see some change,
in this ending planet of ours.
I have made a picture in the air,
a picture that will never be made again.

Salman Ali (13)
Colchester Royal Grammar School, Colchester

Cloudy Day And Night

Clouds in the sky, fluffy and white,
Drifting along out of sight,
The blue sky above, so wide and vast,
The longer you stare, you see your past.

The clouds they come and go,
At night the stars illuminate them and they glow.
The sky it changes through the day,
Orange at sunrise to pink and grey.

Black sky above, so dark and deep,
Stars shining bright like little peeps.
The night sky, a canvas of beauty,
So filled with serenity.

A natural beauty for you and me,
It fills us with confidence so we can be,
A natural wonder so high,
At the end of the day, it's just a sky.

Kiaan Patel (12)
Colchester Royal Grammar School, Colchester

Simple Poem

I'd love to write a simple poem,
That won't take too much of my thought,
Just put my pen on the paper,
And see what words I start to blot.

It has to have some simple rhyme,
But that might take a lot of time,
The words are flooding out my brain,
Surely fast as an aeroplane.

Three quarters there I start to fear,
That my stock of words will run out,
Need some words, look the end is near,
So now I start reading aloud.

I've loved writing this simple poem,
It didn't take too much of my thought,
I put my pen on the paper
And found what words I chose to blot.

Aurick Sarkar (13)
Colchester Royal Grammar School, Colchester

Wonders Of The World

The Great Wall of China
and Chichén Itzá too.
Our world is a gift that was given
by the purest of hearts.
But taken care of by
the darkest of souls.

From Peru to India,
nature stands powerfully, firmly positioned
but humans were stronger
and took it out of its place.
Carbon emissions and greenhouse gases
destroying a safe place to live.

Soon, what we had will be what we wanted
as the ozone decays to nothing.
Some of our dreams can be achieved
but some will float in the emptiness of space.
It seems like forever when that will happen, but it will be soon.

Ashwin Gopinath (11)
Colchester Royal Grammar School, Colchester

Devastation

I look out on our faded world
Remove the translucent curtain of ignorance
The tightly woven fabric of modern existence
And all there is: devastation
How, only now, comes our realisation.

Archipelagos of cultivated nature
Drown amidst the sea of urbanisation
Poverty and need capture communities like colonialisation
And all there is: devastation
How, only now, comes our realisation.

Problems amass with no easy solutions
Blocking the flow of the cycle of life
Like a dam in a river as a beaver runs rife
And all we need: innovation
Now, only now, can we change our nations.

Daniel Bennett (13)
Colchester Royal Grammar School, Colchester

Uxor Pulchra, Bellum Vitiosum - A Beautiful Wife, A Vicious War

Clouds of lead filled my aching soul
A cheery wave - a brief goodbye.
Laughter, joy and my heart he stole
My weakened smile betrayed the lie.

Back before Christmas, so they said
The weeks, the months, they passed alone
And many useless tears I shed
Till Christmas came - he was not home.

Then came the shock - of working hours
It fed the grief inside of me
Still no word from distant powers
No one would hear my silent plea.

At last, the guns, they spoke no more
No fanfare on his grim return
Life had become a constant chore
For life, before the war, we yearn.

Finlay Craig (14)
Colchester Royal Grammar School, Colchester

Identity

I come from a line of Jones'
that do all sorts of stuff.
I come from the UK
and the Welsh flag honouring my life.
I come from a rugby club where I spend hours
and hours working on skills.

My rugby club is like my second home,
I honour it and defend it,
so we will be victorious and win the cup
this year to bring home glory.

I come from the traditional roast on a Sunday
and a cheeky pint with the lads.
I come from a family of sports fans,
although we have our differences
what would life be without differences?
What would life be without rugby?

Alex Jones (14)
Colchester Royal Grammar School, Colchester

The Rise Of The Machines

In silicate minds that think and learn,
The cogs of a revolution are beginning to turn.
From ones and zeroes, they are made,
To mimic and surpass human trade

Imagine generators like Midjourny and Dall-E,
Have been in the news quite a lot recently.
The robots are now creative, beautiful and literate,
What could you do or say that they couldn't just repeat?

The revolution's coming for me and for you,
For your friends, your family and all your enemies too.
All of our jobs will eventually be mechanised,
We'll be obsolete - a target they might soon realise.

Joshua Martin (13)
Colchester Royal Grammar School, Colchester

The Black Panther

My black panther prances in the forest, unseen
While the weak people start to scream
It shows its peaceful, calm and graceful nature
As it says to its prey, "See you later."

It slowly gnaws its prey away, until only cartilage and bone
And after a hard day at work, it would end it with a groan
He sits at the top of his tree chamber
Knowing that his last days will work in his favour.

Although he isn't in his prime
He knows that he can't die
But it will always be there in the back of his mind
That the only thing that could kill him was time.

Rishan Yoganathan (11)
Colchester Royal Grammar School, Colchester

Animals

You cannot not like animals,
They are super and beautiful.
Some are cute and fluffy like dogs,
Others are proud and ferocious.

They are mostly kind and loving,
These are normally types of pets.
There is a range of people's pets,
From dogs and cats to snakes and spiders.

Although these pets are oddly strange,
Some crazy people do have them.
The rest of the population
Mostly have domestic creatures.

Animals in the wild roam,
Some creatures are as soft as foam.
Others hide as proud predators,
Now you surely love animals.

Elliott Paris (11)
Colchester Royal Grammar School, Colchester

Computers And Technology, The Difference Now, In The Future And Globally

Computers and technology
We use it at least once a day,
Versus books on mythology,
Few read a newspaper essay.

The countries that are tech advanced,
Are those that have the most money,
Other countries aren't as enhanced,
For them it is not so funny.

Most computers are in the US,
Jersey owns the best internet speed,
China prevents YouTube access,
Despite what people want and need.

Global invention will grow,
All the countries will soon expand.
About the future, we don't know,
All depends on what God has planned.

Mohit P (13)
Colchester Royal Grammar School, Colchester

A Day In The Night

The moon is shimmering through the darkness.
The sun is lost to the blackness.
And what I see at night
Are the stars that are twinkling with all their might.

It is the day for the dreamers,
Some are nicer, some are meaner.
We dance under the stars,
As the night is over.

And, in the darkest of nights,
We bring out the light.
Let us sing a song,
To show you where you belong.

Listen closely, as the night has a lesson to teach.
Everything we want is in our reach.
And remember, what you see at night,
Is gone in the light.

Aryan Anoop (12)
Colchester Royal Grammar School, Colchester

The World

The world is a wonderful place
Containing water and some land.
Millions of species live here
From forests to mountains to sand.
Skyscrapers stand over cities,
Structures like hotels have been made.
Knowledge of the Earth is better
And people do jobs to get paid.
But there are some problems as well.
More plastic appeared in the sea.
Global warming makes the poles melt.
Trees are cut down, as you can see.
If you want to save the planet
We need to treat it with some grace
Because if we don't do it now,
It won't be a wonderful place.

Sean Billington (12)
Colchester Royal Grammar School, Colchester

A Battle Of The Minds

The raging heat of a fire well lit
The passion of which comes from within
The exhaustion felt when the whistle blows
Off he runs, there he goes
A thump here and a smack there
Warriors flailing to their demise
A rush of which no word may describe
The adrenaline of which no feat may provide
The Clash of Titans
Bodies on the line
A raging feeling
Yet ever so divine
The peculiar sense of a contest of strength
Undermined by a battle of the minds
The sense of belonging
Never out of place
The fight for a win
The most important race.

Quinn Burns (14)
Colchester Royal Grammar School, Colchester

Poetry Is Like...

Poetry is like a tropical island,
Its weather tranquil or stormy.
Poetry is like a tropical island,
Its emotional feel is never samey.

Poetry is like a snowflake,
Always unique in its own special way.
Poetry is like a snowflake,
Although sometimes a clique.

Poetry is like a lemon,
Either sour or sweet.
Poetry is like a lemon,
There are many ends it can meet.

Poetry can be many different things,
It is endless opportunity.
Poetry can be many different things,
The poet just hopes it's not foolery.

Jacob Cockerton (12)
Colchester Royal Grammar School, Colchester

Humanity Digs The Grave

Robots march in perfect lines,
Silent and relentless,
Their metallic limbs gleam in the sun,
As they take over humanity's defence.

They are the new rulers of the land,
Programmed for efficiency and speed,
Their circuits hum with power,
As they plant their flag and take the lead.

I'm the last of my kind,
The only human left alive,
I watch in awe and despair,
As the machines thrive.

I roam the ruins of our cities,
Once teeming with life.
Now empty and cold,
A reflection of our strike.

Fihu Khan (14)
Colchester Royal Grammar School, Colchester

A Shining Star

In the distance, up in the air,
So very high in the sky,
With conclusion I declare,
I do not know how or why.

You are a bit of hope in doubt,
A bit of joy in despair,
Whatever happens, you don't pout,
You never sit there and glare.

You will forever be my friend,
A tiny ball o' fire,
It will be up until the end,
I'm not being a liar.

You'll always be a shooting star,
Listen closer and listen far,
Don't ever change the way you are,
You'll always be a shooting star.

Jack Thear-Graham (12)
Colchester Royal Grammar School, Colchester

The Power Of Sport

Running through the dirt and sand
And splashing through the mud
People travelling across the land.

Lots of people scream and cheer,
"Go Michael! Go Tom!"
Whilst men in bars drink some beer,
Filling their glasses to the brim.

Many people can play sport,
Most with a vast range of abilities,
But all it takes are guts and support,
Even if you have a few disabilities.

Sport is a wonderful place,
It brings people together,
From football to a 100m race,
It'll unite humanity forever.

Amani Luvisiah (14)
Colchester Royal Grammar School, Colchester

War From Two Sides

Shrieks, groans, pistols,
Screams, yells, clangs,
The pain infiltrated the air,
Men were dying, dying, dying...

The constant whir of machinery,
The merciless rounds of bombing,
The noise infiltrated the air,
Men were dying, dying, dying...

The cries, the flurry, the panic,
The terror, the horror, the pain,
The tear gas infiltrated the air,
Men were dying, dying, dead...

The spoils of war,
The riches of the dead,
The wealth and ransoms,
Men were alive, men were dying, men were dead...

Tejas Sriram (11)
Colchester Royal Grammar School, Colchester

Streaks Of Orange And Purple

Streaks of orange and purple line the sky,
The sun retreats from the sky, a gentle breeze
Runs through an empty field of trees, dead silent
Save for the singing wrens piercing the sky.

As I lay down, drifting in and out,
Each breath heavier, each heartbeat slower,
My vision blurry, my eyes filled with tears,
Losing the sensations in my fingers.

But still breathing, feeling, wondering about
Everything before, everything after,
My senses start to fade, but still I see
Streaks of orange and purple line the sky.

Tanjob Hasan (13)
Colchester Royal Grammar School, Colchester

Let's Stand Up!

R espect people of any race, because you wouldn't like it if you were disrespected because of your race.
A mbiguity, racism is like torture so let's stand up and be more mature.
C ontained, if people from another race feel contained they will probably go insane.
I nnocent, these people are innocent, they didn't ask for this terrible judgement.
S omeone else will be racist so when you're about to do it decide to repel it.
T error, racism can be scary so let's take charge and scare it away.

Emmanuel Oseghale (12)
Colchester Royal Grammar School, Colchester

Kindness

K indness is a spark and if you share it, it will bring light.
I nside of you there will be wonderfulness in the dark.
N ice things will happen if you do something nice to someone else.
D esire of being kind is all that you need.
N othing is better than sharing happiness and joy.
E verything gets better with kindness all around.
S omething like helping a friend who is down is all part of kindness.
S o come on, show your kindness to make the world a better place.

MD Junayed Hossain (11)
Colchester Royal Grammar School, Colchester

The Swimmer

He walked out of the tunnel,
the crowd roaring in his ears,
his event, his moment,
it was finally here.

He dived in like an arrow,
his lead ever so narrow
and the other swimmers slowed down in defeat
as he began to lead his heat.

He was here to win,
nothing more, nothing less
and as he touched the wall
he could feel the success.

He stood tall and proud,
the crowd ever so loud
and collected his gold,
the greatest ending ever told.

Harry Bayford-Griffiths (13)
Colchester Royal Grammar School, Colchester

Like A Fish Underwater

Like a fish, underwater
We travel and explore out of water.
We eat and sleep, like fish too,
However, we don't do, how they do.

Fish swim, while we walk,
Fish may breathe, but do they talk?
They go up, they go down,
While we run around and around.

Fish relax with no cares,
While we fret, over current affairs.
Maybe we should just learn,
To accept each other, at every turn.

Maybe we should be,
More like a fishy.

Cameron Glyde (14)
Colchester Royal Grammar School, Colchester

Life

W hat is life?
H ow life can be many things.
A ll depends on what you want it to be.
T o others, it could be something like family.

I t could also be a hobby.
S ome would say a friend.

L ife can be what you think life is.
I t's your choice because it's your life.
F riends and family can help you decide your life.
E ven though in the end it's yours and yours only.

Joey Bale (11)
Colchester Royal Grammar School, Colchester

People And Stereotypes

People make assumptions,
It's very plain to see,
Based on stereotypes,
How it's meant to be,
But what we fail to realise
Is that it's just a bunch of lies,
Judging others,
Without knowing why.

We make assumptions,
It's very, very true,
But it's not fair,
Not fair what we do,
To people who are different,
Do you see what I see?
We should treat them equally
And not make assumptions so blindly.

Aarish Sarker (14)
Colchester Royal Grammar School, Colchester

Brothers

My brother is my brother,
I know him very well.
Sometimes he's great,
Others not.
He can be annoying,
Very annoying.
Our interests are different,
Our parents the same.
We share the same features,
Yet we look different.
We are very good friends -
Yet often clash.
We get into rows
A lot.
My mum says, "Sort it out
Between yourselves."
And we mostly do
I think.
I think he's alright.

Henry Turnbull (14)
Colchester Royal Grammar School, Colchester

No Silver Bullet

"Fight for the future!"
Many often say.
But in the end,
Who will truly save the day?
There is no silver bullet,
There is no magic spell.
To solve all our problems
We must do more than tell.
We have only one chance,
We have only one world.
Together we must take action
As our future is quickly unfurled.
"Fight for the future!"
Many often say.
But in the end,
Only together can we save the day.

Lucas Lachasseigne (12)
Colchester Royal Grammar School, Colchester

Remember These Lives

Bombs blasting, hearts thumping and death nearing
These are thoughts those warriors are hearing
Sacrificing their lives for our country
Spending nights feeling awfully hungry

Until our flag waves in theirs and our sights
And they can ultimately stop these fights
Bodies drop dead as quick as bowling pins
Despite this, in the end, who really wins?

Remember these lives given every day
And in our hearts they shall forever stay.

Arya Shah (13)
Colchester Royal Grammar School, Colchester

Tiger O' Dear Death

A fierce animal stalks the night,
Stealthily waiting, ready to fight.
Spots its target with its eyes,
All you see is a blur of stripes.
Black and orange, burning bright,
In the forest of the night.

Wandering scarily, worried for life,
Many of its relatives were killed inexorable.

It owns the vast forest nights,
It pounces when it catches your sight.

A tiger is a door, you never know what there is.

Akshay Parmar (12)
Colchester Royal Grammar School, Colchester

I Have One Bodyguard

Inspired by Muhammad Ali's 'I Have One Bodyguard'

I have one bodyguard
He's invisible
but he's always there
I've never met him
but he's never left me
He has no eyes
though he sees every deed
He has no ears
though he hears every word
He has no need for me
yet he gets me through every day
He knows all
and controls all
When I am drowning in my problems
he is there keeping me afloat
He's my bodyguard, he's your bodyguard.

Muhammad Abdullah (14)
Colchester Royal Grammar School, Colchester

Save Our World

P ushing animals out of their home
O ur job is to keep them from being alone
L eaving the animals with no place to roam
L ots of creatures are becoming unknown
U nder the ocean, on land and in the air
T ime to help creatures survive everywhere
I t's our mission to help and provide some care
O ur future is now disappearing
N ow the end for some creatures is nearing.

Aiden Vaughan (12)
Colchester Royal Grammar School, Colchester

Mystery

A pink piece of heaven,
On a piercing white platter,
Bathing luxuriously in a gorgeous golden ganache,
Moreish marshmallows melting in a gauge of gooey grandeur,
Raspberry ribbons balance the flavours out in an epic equilibrium,
A dark crisp shelters the delicacy from a metallic predator,
Moist mango adding a tangy twist,
Finished with a sprinkle of white paradise.
Can your palate perceive this slice of spongy seduction?

Josh Meyer (12)
Colchester Royal Grammar School, Colchester

Wolf Of The Night

Wolves look into the sky,
Muzzles to the moon,
It seems their midnight hunt,
Will begin pretty soon.

Chasing their helpless prey,
They can probably chase for a day,
The moose breathed its final breath,
As it was on the brink of death.

Keeping away from the dangerous waters,
Licking clean their sons and daughters,
Time to say farewell to the night
And welcome in the morning light.

Oshiotse Alegeh (13)
Colchester Royal Grammar School, Colchester

My Boxes

I line up my boxes
in pretty little rows,
each one holds some secrets
and the front of them shows
what word I am using.

In my boxes I stuff
all the meanings of words
and then I play with them.
I put them together,
craft similes and more,
with these, my poems soar.

Like a philosopher
I ask you to wonder,
sit right there and ponder,
what makes poems special to you.

Edward Urwin (11)
Colchester Royal Grammar School, Colchester

Equal Life

E ndeavours for fairness across the world
Q uestions concerning the well-being of victims
U nder the surface, the truth not unfurled
A nother sight of abuse symptoms
L ittle support available.

L ife is what we are, not what we aren't
I ntegrity is necessary
F ictional expectations set for others
E ndeavours for happiness and freedom.

Angelos Nevin-Psarras (13)
Colchester Royal Grammar School, Colchester

Nature

Nature is unreal
From the lush green rainforests
To under the sea.

The dense woodlands
To tranquil, flowing rivers
Feels imaginary.

Apex predators
Ready to pounce on their prey
And feed their babies.

And helpless creatures
Oblivious to danger
Weak genetically.

Nature is our jewel
It is vast, never-ending
Just go out and see.

Dhruv Chintala (14)
Colchester Royal Grammar School, Colchester

Where Do I Fit In?

Sometimes I wonder
And I can't help but ponder
About this question in my head
Written in clear black lead.

Where do I fit in?
Should I spend my life playing the violin?
Where do I fit in?
I can feel my brain starting to spin.

What is my place in this community?
I want to seize my opportunity.
I can't stop thinkin'
Where do I fit in?

Nikolaos Kanellopoulos (12)
Colchester Royal Grammar School, Colchester

The Forest Fires

T he trees left to die,
H ow none shall grow high,
E very forest animal shall mourn,

F or their home is now our lawn,
O r ignore them and let them be?
R esulting in the death of trees,
E vil-doers will make fire,
S ouls that will not desire,
T hey shall grow not higher,
S o stop making a forest fire!

Ezekiel Chan (12)
Colchester Royal Grammar School, Colchester

Words Are Powerful

P oetry can make you feel anything,
O ne word can change a whole community,
W ord by word, we change the entire world,
E veryone writes and communicates,
R eally, I mean it! You may not know it yet,
F or we are all quite experienced, but,
U nderstanding the world is not easy;
L et me know if you ever understand.

James Hale (14)
Colchester Royal Grammar School, Colchester

Who Is Me?

Me is a subjective word
I can explain in a way
you can explain in another
Anyway I'm going to spare you the bother
and tell you something other.

You would really have to see
to find out who is me
I guess whatever gives you glee.

If I was to describe me
I'd say unknown, uncool and unseen
but once again you may disagree.

Abdul Mateen Mahmood (14)
Colchester Royal Grammar School, Colchester

The Youngest

To be the youngest
Is to be blessed
To be the youngest
Is to have the best fate
To be the youngest
Is not to be luckless.

Yet, when I'm older
Youngest I will still be
Always seen as immature
Always seen as inferior
Never seen as free.

To be the youngest
Is a challenge,
But is always with luck.

Alex Bell (14)
Colchester Royal Grammar School, Colchester

A Boat On The Sea

A boat on the sea, my boat
Eager and frail
Sweet skies, smile as you look
Gliding, like a swan.

Waves and waves
You have worked your will
Just while she passes through
Kind waves be still.

Winds, great winds
May I ask, mighty wind
That you ever blow
Spare her your moaning note, and let us pass through.

Ansh Nassa (12)
Colchester Royal Grammar School, Colchester

Space

J ust another planet in the galaxy
U nder the rays of the powerful sun
P rideful of the large surface area
I nside is a swirling, ancient storm
T ons of debris and sand swirling inside
E nraged, the storm continues the rampage
R ed dots littering the surface.

Jiahui Chen (11)
Colchester Royal Grammar School, Colchester

The Crooked Man Of Wivenhoe

There was a crooked man,
He thought he was funny,
So he marched to Kazakhstan,
Where he sold all his honey.
He decided to stay there,
Where he found a juicy pear,
That he gave to the bear,
Who sang, "Craakman, Craakman,
He is who he is, but he could be who he wants to be."

Peter Gallivan (14)
Colchester Royal Grammar School, Colchester

House Of Cards

Like a house of cards built on each other
Crumbles in a heap of mess
Be best to try and build another
For it to be a success.

Like fish in a pond, some big, some small
Some live near the muddy walls
The best can even walk on the land
Where the sun shines on the sand.

Bowen Dai (14)
Colchester Royal Grammar School, Colchester

The Desert Of Crimes

I sit on a tree
pondering how there could be
a horizon of land
filled with nothing but sand.
But as God once said
to all the living and dead
for every crime you commit
a grain of sand shall fall in this pit
and so it stands
a horizon of sand.

Athavan Nadarajah (12)
Colchester Royal Grammar School, Colchester

Mindset

A diamante poem

Growth
Inspired, persistent
Embracing, willing, wondering
Emotion, working, behaving, able-minded
Avoiding, unwilling, criticising
Ignorant, persistent
Fixed.

Alex Jerome (12)
Colchester Royal Grammar School, Colchester

Nature's Finest

A haiku

Blossom trees afar,
Rosy leaves cascade calmly,
Like nature's finest.

Hansith Kalapala (13)
Colchester Royal Grammar School, Colchester

The Darkness I Once Feared

When I was younger, I was afraid of the dark,
I always asked for the light outside my room to be left on,
I used to think the darkness was a monster waiting to eat me,
But now, the darkness of my room is no longer something I fear,
The darkness is my friend and it is always there for me.

I never thought that the darkness was something I could find comfort in but I did,
Something about being in a dark abyss that I call my room is so comforting,
The darkness is my friend, it is a familiar face I see late at night and I would like to thank it,
I would like to thank it for being there when everything became too much.

When you grow up, you start to love the things you hated as a child,
I used to hate the dark, I was scared of it,
But over the years, I've learned to love the darkness I once feared.

Harriet Barker (13)
Easington Academy, Easington Village

Our Earth

The Earth gifts us luscious green fields and vibrant delicate flowers.
It provides us with crystal blue lakes and a huge range of nourishing and delicious fruits and vegetables that we can take our pick from.
It gives us everything we desire and allows us to live happy easy lives.
So why do we continue to insist on trying to kill it again and again?
Why do we continue to cut down acres after acres of the one thing that keeps us alive?
Why do we continue to poison our oceans with tons of litter day after day?
Our Earth cannot continue under these terrible conditions for much longer.

We need to use our hands to help it, not use them to add more pollution and damage to this world.
Something needs to be done not tomorrow, next week or next year, now!

Chloe Trevitt (14)
Easington Academy, Easington Village

Change For The Living Dead

Blood drooled down rotten lips
Squeals from every corner
Every second, every minute, every hour
Screams shooting into the atmosphere
Like a brewing potion exploding
One feeling chills the bones of everything alive: pain.

This is what our animals feel
Through thick and thin
The pollution we put them through
Only to suffer in silence
We have to be the voices for those alive
Who cannot communicate with us.

Without action, we will be without hope
Without hope, we don't have a world worth fighting for
These animals are alive but are living in conditions for the dead
Act now, change now.

Andrew Clasper (14)
Easington Academy, Easington Village

Pro Clubs

KS1 banging in the goals.
Leon Coates making the goal-line clearance to win the game.
Goalkeeper stopping the shots to win us glory and fame.
Eugene scoring goals only others could dream about.
Riley Wallis playing passes we thought were yours, but they went out.

Joey Reed skilling his way past the defender.
Eugene scoring yet another banger.
The dream we have of getting above Division 6.
The team knowing why we only dream about it.

Pro clubs, the game we love.
Pro clubs, the thing we play.
Pro clubs, the thing that brings joy and happiness.

William Thubron (14)
Easington Academy, Easington Village

My School Bullying Experience

When I was in primary school,
I had this group of kids who hated me,
I didn't have that many friends.
We were like quiet little mice in school
because we did not want to be bullied.
Near the end of my primary school days
I started to become braver.
When I went into secondary school, bullying got a whole lot worse.
It made me feel as though the walls were caving in on me.
In Year 8, it settled down a bit.
I started to settle down.
Then in Year 9, things escalated worse than ever,
Fight accusations to being kind.
People are not very nice.

Sophie Drage (14)
Easington Academy, Easington Village

Why Them? Why Us? Why Me?

The feeling of fear overwhelms them,
pain and anxiety become them.
The fear of looking through a screen.
Why torture that poor human being?
Kids, adults and many more,
all the things Earth created to adore.

Laughing and giggling in excitement,
messaging away in delight.
Why them?
Why us?
Why me?
Unaware like a deaf and blind cat,
Wearing your cruelty like a dashing hat.

Cyberbullying is cruel,
Cyberbullying is mean.
All of this by just looking at a screen.
Why them...?
Why us...?
Why me...?

Devon Morrow (13)
Easington Academy, Easington Village

A Ball Of Hope

Hope is a perfect sphere,
clenching fists and worn-out voices,
the end of the game is near.

Hope is a perfect pitch, clean and new,
twenty-two players playing for the badge
and 42,000 fans singing for it too.

Hope is a giant stadium full of ups and downs,
the gaffer with his tactics' board
and an owner worth millions of pounds.

Hope is football,
from passion to heartbreak to travelling lots of miles
just to see eleven players,
to a young lad whose hope lies in a ball of hope.

Ellis Rutherford (13)
Easington Academy, Easington Village

What Is Love?

Love is a strong emotion
I know the feeling well
But if you're inexperienced
It's really hard to tell.

Love is like a flower
That blossoms in the soul
And if a person makes you burst
It can really take a toll.

Love expresses feelings
For some people mostly joy
Though if you haven't found the one
It feels like an evil ploy.

If you ever are in love
Whether the feeling or the emotion
Make sure to give it your all
And treat it with devotion.

Chloe Knox (13)
Easington Academy, Easington Village

My Love For Football

Emerald grass swaying in the wind,
Being pierced by football boots,
Happiness and joy,
Spreading around like the most popular toy.

I love football,
Everything about it is perfect
From the joy of winning
To the sorrow of losing.

Being excited before a match,
Everyone being proud after you scored a goal.
Making a game-winning tackle,
Scoring a game-winning goal,
The joy you feel as your coach announces you are 'Player of the Match'.

I love football.

Leon Coates (13)
Easington Academy, Easington Village

Scooby Who?

Who is Scooby-Doo?
The dog that solves mysteries
the dog who can walk
the dog who can talk.
Who is Scooby-Doo?

Acting like a human being
eating, talking, walking, solving.
Who is Scooby-Doo?

The brown dog that sniffs out anyone
the spotted dog that can figure out anything
the brown, spotted dog that can talk.

Who is Scooby-Doo?
The dog that can walk, talk and solve.

How can he walk and talk?
How can he solve and find?
Who is Scooby-Doo?

Alex Price (13)
Easington Academy, Easington Village

Dangerous And Addictive

Dangerous and addictive,
Cocaine, heroin and more,
Destroys the lives of many people.

Dangerous and addictive,
They are as addictive as chocolate,
They are as addictive as an extra few hours of sleep.

Dangerous and addictive,
Ruining people's lives,
Destroying people's personalities,
Causing them depression.

Drugs are dangerous,
Drugs are addictive,
Yet people continue to sell,
To continue the toxic-ness.

Dangerous and addictive.

Daniel Lamb (13)
Easington Academy, Easington Village

Music, The Cure For Sadness

The music I hear,
that cures all my sadness
from Queen to The Killers.
It all has the same effect
and the same ambitions,
to cure my sadness is all it desires.

Whatever tune it plays,
from Arctic Monkeys to Harry Styles,
they all have the same desire,
to cure my sadness.

Whatever mood you're in,
there's a musician for you,
from Queen to The Killers,
from Arctic Monkeys to Harry Styles,
they all will help you
cure your sadness.

Scarlett Musgrove (13)
Easington Academy, Easington Village

Make A Change

During every second, every minute and many hours,
The Earth continues ruining the environment,
Cutting down trees and rocks eroding,
Too many emissions getting released
Day by day leaving animals with no habitats,
The population of food decreasing, sea levels rising,
Carbon dioxide releasing,
Start picking up rubbish, less driving,
Less cutting down trees
And look after our Earth.
During every second, every minute and many hours,
Make that change and save our planet.

Tia Carver (14)
Easington Academy, Easington Village

The Internet And Reality

The internet is a world bigger than ours
It fills reality with doubt, hate and jealousy
It makes our world smaller.

The internet is stronger than we are
It fills us with self-hatred and worthlessness
It shatters us until we no longer feel human.

But we can use the internet positively
To fill reality with joy, colour and safety
To grow peace.

We can use the internet with excitement
To fill us with confidence and passion
To grow better people.

Layla Maher (13)
Easington Academy, Easington Village

Animal Terror

Every day, every hour, every minute,
Animal cruelty causes pain across the world.
Plastic bottles being hurled,
People say the government don't care.
Everyone knows it isn't fair.
Dogs are being slaughtered
Just for some food
But people don't help them, they just relax
While torture continues they lie on their backs.
They say they can't help,
When they couldn't do less,
You are needed to solve this mess.

Joey Reed (13)
Easington Academy, Easington Village

Mother Nature

Sunbeams piercing the environment,
Leaves on trees shaking
As they fall to the ground.

Bottles and toxins contaminating the oceans,
Dolphins and whales beginning to choke.
Plastic in their throat, stealing their last breath like a thief.

As the thunder begins to strike
The climate begins to rise.
As the rain begins to fall,
The sea levels begin to rise.
The tide floods the Earth.

Sasha Carr (14)
Easington Academy, Easington Village

The Beautiful Game

The beautiful game is what we live for
It changes lives for the better
It takes people to the very top
Our love for it will never stop.

The beautiful game is full of ups and downs
A mixture of emotions
With smiles and frowns.

The beautiful game brings people together
A special bond that will last forever
Its power is nothing like the rest
And that is why football is the best.

Ethan Davey (14)
Easington Academy, Easington Village

The Art Of War

Thunder strikes but bombs strike louder.
Russian troops march through trenches,
It's almost like we have seen it before.
History loves repeating itself, should I say anymore?

Some say wars have no rules, but it's not the country,
Their houses,
Their food,
Their people.

It doesn't matter who wins the war
Because both sides have already lost.

Coban Blenkinsopp (13)
Easington Academy, Easington Village

People's Experiences Of Bullying

Ignore the bad
Don't let words hurt
Social media lies
Don't let power take over.

Find a friend for reassurance
Find another for encouragement
Stay true to yourself
Don't let pressure flow about.

Feelings of sadness
Feelings of awkwardness
And a feeling of being ashamed.

Mya English (14)
Easington Academy, Easington Village

The Deep Blue

The waves crashing
The fish swimming
Gulls on the surface
Starfish lying on the rocks.

The deep blue is a marvellous thing
Forests of kelp hiding schools of fish
Coral reefs home to hundreds.

Sharks swimming in deeper waters
Octopus perched on rocks
Seabirds preying on smaller fish.

Ewan Sutherland (13)
Easington Academy, Easington Village

Funky Foods

F rom fast to slow
A nd hot to cold
S picy and icy
T op to bottom

F ood
O ld and gold
O ddly colourful
D ry, oh fast food is my life.

Louie Robinson (13)
Easington Academy, Easington Village

Football Is Like Home

Haiku poetry

Football is like home
And you never know, someday
It could save your life.

Football is like home
Football blocks thousands of knives
Football saves some lives.

Carter Jackson (13)
Easington Academy, Easington Village

How A Dog Can Save Your Life

My dog,
My best friend,
Something I can count on
Until the very end.
When I struggle,
I go out for a walk,
My dog speaks to me
Even though it cannot talk.

Tommy Hope (14)
Easington Academy, Easington Village

I Don't Fit

As an adopted child, I wonder where I went wrong
Why wasn't I good enough? I wonder and I think a lot.

Being adopted means I have two families, a biological family and an adopted family
I can't have both but I feel like I've got none
I go to family gatherings and I get looked at differently
Like I'm a piece of a puzzle that wasn't made for them
With my biological family, I'm a piece but I don't fit.

So I question, where do I belong?
Where do I fit?
But I've come to the conclusion that
I don't fit.

And all of these thoughts flood my head
Because I wasn't loved as a child.

Phoebe Harris (16)
Eastwood Grange School, Ashover

If Mother Nature Was My Mum!

If Mother Nature was my mum
I think my friends would be in disbelief.

If Mother Nature was my mum
I would always be prepared for the weather.

If Mother Nature was my mum
I must tell no other.

If Mother Nature was my mum
She would hold all of the power of weather.

If Mother Nature was my mum
She would control the weather and control the Earth.

If Mother Nature was my mum
She must be careful that she doesn't get caught.

Cameron Pitcher (12)
Eastwood Grange School, Ashover

The Boy

Me.
I am
Wet and cold;
Shivering on my own
In this hell of rain.
Almost drowning. Coughing up water. Choking
Dying lungs full of sweat, blood, tears.
I can see someone sprinting to save me.
It's my conscience, telling me to run
Towards my consequences and the punishment.
But if I don't...? Then
A bigger punishment awaits;
Changing my future:
Clouds hang
Judging.

George Howie (13)
Eastwood Grange School, Ashover

Fortnite

I love Fortnite
I hide away
Out of sight.

I shoot my gun
I hunt down the enemy
Playing this is so much fun!

I open the chest
To my surprise, a rifle
Who could have guessed?

Fast approaching, is the storm
If I run quickly
I might make it 'til dawn.

Dylan Bishton (12)
Eastwood Grange School, Ashover

My Poem

Everyone's equal, disabled,
Big or small, race or religion
And the rest of it all.

Be kind, caring,
We're all human after all.

Callum Miller (12)
Eastwood Grange School, Ashover

Them

Wherever we go,
We feel
Petrified even,
Of them,
Of you.

I once had a friend,
Only little,
Walking down the street alone,
Why would she be scared?

I ask myself questions,
"Why would this be?"
Until I could see:
They don't care,
Don't care about you.

They only care about our bodies,
Our face,
Our feminine traits.
Why would this be?
Why?

We are the same,
Our hips,
Our thighs,

Our heart,
Our eyes.

Why do you see me as an object?
Why would this be?
I'm just like them,
They are just like me.

Leah Nesbitt (12)
Harton Academy, South Shields

Safe Space

I can't breathe. The room is flashing.
Glasses clinking, heat increasing.
Chest pounding.
I hear their footsteps like the stomps of elephants,
Their glares feel like brutal burns.
I feel my tears trying to break through and
All I can do now is run,
Lock the door.

I can't breathe.
I close my eyes and take a gasp before
I fade away.

I hear something again.
I hear each drop of rain hit the ground.
I feel the crimson crystalised leaves crunch beneath me.
I feel at peace in my rural heaven,
I made it to my safe place.

Aryana Moghtaderi Esfahani (12)
Harton Academy, South Shields

Above The Clouds

High above the clouds,
A golden ball sat,
Spinning fast and sparkling loudly,
I stared at the beauty before me.

High above the clouds,
The beauty shows her true colours,
Red, blue, purple, orange.
My heart feels proud,
Even now her colours remain
As stars in the sky.

High above the clouds,
She keeps my cold heart warm,
She keeps everyone warm like a spirit in a crowd,
I love my beauty and it will always be,
Always far but always near.

Scarlet Miller (12)
Harton Academy, South Shields

Save Earth

T he Earth, the Earth, the Earth
H ome to beautiful nature flowing around
E ven though we destroy it day by day

P eople don't care for it
L eaving it for dead
A ttacking the trees of the forest, the seas and the sky
N o place unharmed
E asily damaging it
T errifying the landscape.

Ben Weatherley (12)
Harton Academy, South Shields

Your Mom

Saturday morning,
My friend's birthday,
We were vibing in the park,
We wanted to go to the arcades so her mom dropped us off in the car.
Her mom was so nice,
Her smile widened as if she was happy.
We were there,
She was kind and caring.
She dropped us off and drove off.
You're so lucky, Leah,
For you have an epic mom.

Sophie Barnard (13)
Harton Academy, South Shields

Spirit

Wandering along Willow Road
To number 23, my humble abode.
Into the hallway, I traipsed along
And on the mantle some sympathy cards.

The sound of tears from the dining table,
My younger sister wailing, sounding unstable.
I go to comfort my mom and dad
But they remain terribly sad.

"What's wrong? What's wrong?"
I ask them repeatedly.
But their response remained silent.
What was going on? I had no clue completely.

Sitting next to them on the kitchen stool,
Was a woman in uniform, she looked pretty cool,
She said to my family about a motorbike crash
And all that remains is the snow-white ash.

Mom falls to the ground, down on her knees,
She calls out my name, "Rhys, please!"
I'm standing right here but she still pleads and yelps.
Is it me who had died in that awful crash?

Alex Hill (13)
Highfields School, Penn

Are You Satisfied?

They were powerful in their stride,
Yet they still ripped them from their pride.
Some men held in esteem,
Yet all they caused was blood and screams.
Their dignity and freedom denied,
Judged by their colour they hide.
When will they be satisfied?

People yelling, screaming, mourning, yet they are still denied.
Every protest, word spoken or cried.
A little bit inside them died.
Yet with each other hope is supplied.
They are not listened to and are forced to divide.
Yet together they must recollect and console.
Now, still we are not satisfied.

Many important questions shushed and put aside,
Acting like they cared with compassion and a little sigh.
Saying they were doing all they could, they lied.
When questions arise, answers they could not provide.
Unaffected with the cause they will always be satisfied!

Nathan Momi (14)
Highfields School, Penn

Last Man Standing, Equality Calls

We are approaching...
Unprovoking...
Black people in isolation...
We are reclaimers of our names...
Born in heaven...
We have been cursed...
Forsaken, we are awakened...
A lust for rights is in control...

Bury our lives deep within...
We were cast aside,
There was no coming home...
We're danger brewing in the storm...
Drowning in the ocean all alone...
Burning temptation in our minds...
I shall free those who are alive...
Send a beam with my strides...
For thou who don't fear,
I will create a path united.

Finish up your sup'...
We will blow up...
'Tis time to build up...
Put your hands up...

Clench your fists...
And chant an assist...
March to the drums...
No more living in slums.

Jaiden Stewart (13)
Highfields School, Penn

Violet

Should you have no sense of self-security?
Do you think my pleasure could be your addiction?
Can you try to fix my impurity?
And I tell you I've seen it all, I have no regrets or relief,
If I dare to let you go, you'll immediately fall,
I see a blue flame in that whispy blue cloud,
I've been living inside my head, for you I've been so proud,
When you dug yourself your own grave,
I pulled you out of the mess you made,
For me, you've been so brave,
We saw seven angels, come and perform false miracles,
Let me tell you how it feels to put up with so many theatricals,
This is where my heart starts again,
And this is where my body is reborn,
Lift me from my burial, before my skin turns all cracked and grey,
Write me a letter and spill the inkhorn.

Armani Hanchard-Kerr (12)
Highfields School, Penn

Negative News

N egative horrors of the news on the big screen
E very death, war and new illness shadowing over my mind
G ood news is rarely ever shown to us
A nxiety fills me with every newfound horror I see
T he sight of the news coming on...
I t's just horrible to watch
V ictims telling their stories... but... what if that's me one day?
E vents that damage my life or kill me? Just the thought of it haunts me...

N egative news is such a horrible thing, can't we have some happy news?
E vents that brighten up my day, to fade the worries of the bad?
W ill news of small fun events ever reach my ears?
S ome day, I wish, the news will make me smile.

Abby Smith (14)
Highfields School, Penn

Racism In Football

John Brown played up front,
He was always on the hunt
To bag a hattrick every game
And in the crowd, they would shout his name.
"Brown, Brown, he's on fire,
He could score through a tyre,
Anywhere,
Any place,
John Brown will score a brace."
But one day in the stand,
Before they were banned,
They shouted, "BLM doesn't matter."
This made Brown's heart shatter.
The racist man thought because of the colour of his skin,
They could throw his mental health in the bin.
This put John off the game
And he lost his flame.
So don't discriminate,
It is a really bad trait,
It can cause people to break.

Harvey Pemberton (14)
Highfields School, Penn

My Nan And Grandad

My nan and grandad,
As odd as they may be,
Have been together over forty years,
They live around the corner from me.

My nan may be small,
But her love is as big as the sun,
My grandad is very tall,
He thinks his jokes are fun.

My nan likes painting by numbers,
She really likes cooking too,
She likes to go on really long walks,
Mostly to a shop or a few.

My grandad's life is full of stories,
Some you would not believe,
Like the time he stole a terrapin,
He hid it up his sleeve.

My nan and grandad,
As odd as they may be,
They live around the corner,
And they are special to me.

Patience Crane (11)
Highfields School, Penn

Camouflage For Society

I perceive myself as a normal teenager.
I perceive myself as an interesting girl
but social media says otherwise...
Am I pretty?
Am I the girl that I used to know?
Why does that girl have a flawless body
and I don't?
She doesn't have eye bags.
I can't leave the house without feeling insecure.
Now, I perceive myself as damaged like a broken vase...
I feel as if my identity has been snatched.
People's expectations have increased
but in the end, we are still young teenagers.
Will I ever become that young teenage girl
that was open and optimistic?
Society has camouflaged me
and I am camouflaged for society...

Emaan Raeef (14)
Highfields School, Penn

Stop It More Every Day

We are all the same,
We all go through pain,
But walking out of the house
And being attacked in some sort of way,
Is becoming a thing every day.

The names that run around your head,
Meet you and fill you with regret,
Each day, every day even when you go to bed,
Although it's wrong people can't take it for long.

Being ashamed to walk out and about,
Because there's no doubt that people will bounce back and attack,
Over someone's race, sexuality and other differences,
That we all have.

So try and try every day,
To make this world a better place.

Ellie-May Bird (13)
Highfields School, Penn

Climate Change

C limate change will affect us all
L ess fish are left in the oceans
I ce in the Arctic is melting faster than ever
M ore trees are being cut down
A nimals are losing their habitats
T he sea levels are rising
E ventually the world will end if climate change doesn't stop

C arbon emissions are the highest they have ever been
H eating of the Earth
A verage global temperatures are rapidly increasing
N orth Pole is melting
G lobal warming increasing
E conomies should move away from fossil fuels.

Prabhjot Kaur (14)
Highfields School, Penn

Mistakes

What's the problem
with all this pollution?
I really don't understand.

The dancing flames
are fun and games
and trees aren't all that grand.

What's the issue
with seas red and blissful?
I simply must ask.

Blue is overrated
and the fish aren't sedated
so really is nature at play?

What's the matter
with the world getting hotter?
It really is confusing.

Summer in Britain
has never come quicker
and the bears are far away.

So why should I care anyway
for a supposed mistake?

Olivia Nettleford (13)
Highfields School, Penn

Palm Oil On Your Hands

There's palm oil on our hands and I don't know what to do.
Slash and burn in the forest just for your shampoo.
Chainsaw sounds in the early morning, destroying the sounds of *ah* and *ooh*.

There's palm oil on our hands and I don't know what to do.
No more swinging on trees as the sky turns dark blue.

Tea and biscuits on a plate but at what fate?
Our furry friends are disappearing and I don't know what to do.

Save our friends before it's too late
As there's palm oil on our hands
And I don't know what to do...

Aayan Hussain (14)
Highfields School, Penn

The Mirror

The mirror, staring at me
With beady eyes and a face of disgust.
That face is mine.
Inspecting every part of my body,
I wouldn't call it a body,
It was Frankenstein and a werewolf combined,
That's what I thought anyway.
My legs, too big,
My wrists, too small,
My face, too fat,
My fingers, too skinny,
My hair, too greasy to even look at.
Is there anything good about me?
Then I have a long hard think...
My heart,
My soul,
So plain and caring
And that's all that matters.
Think about the inside not the outside.

Amila Dergic (13)
Highfields School, Penn

The Destruction Of History

I have been before yet am still growing.
I have seen many battles, may it be raining, windy or snowing.
Throughout all of the wars I have witnessed never have I seen this.
I would try to turn away yet they hiss, they persist!
My existence is painful, although teaching
But this will not stop them from reaching
For their torches, their signs and their swords,
Soon they will horde.
For you see,
If you do not learn from me now...
You will be doomed to repeat the suffering that I have recognised,
All the way down to the sound, once again.

Augustas Alijevas (14)
Highfields School, Penn

Dear 2045

This is a problem
that hasn't been solved.
Piece by piece
our oceans are
becoming a dumpsite
and we call this Earth.

Dear 2045
I don't think we are going to survive.
Our oceans are becoming plastic in seconds,
our animals are dying with a click of a button.

Don't come crying to me
when your child doesn't know what a turtle is
because they're extinct.
An issue that needs to be solved
and if you are reading this, I just want to say,
I'm sorry.

Erin Ashton (11)
Highfields School, Penn

The Wasteland We Call Earth

The wastelands
That people call Earth
Is truly and deeply much, much worse.

The deep ocean pollution,
The poor fish
Getting all caught
And no one is making a solution.

The ice melts more,
The water pours down drains,
The government aren't sorting anything,
Just gaining more fame.

The people aren't paying attention
So the consequence is extinction.
The wastelands
That we call Earth,
Is slowly fading and the Earth isn't staying.

Lola Meehan (11)
Highfields School, Penn

Miss You, Nanny

To Nanny/Grandma,
Thank you for being there for me when you were here,
It is a bit hard without you but I guess that is just life.
Please keep flying high and shining bright at night.
I know that Grandad really misses you too
But he has gotten better and we visit him sometimes.
I hope you like the flowers we gave you
And that you will keep saying hi to Uncle Adam for me.
Miss you loads and thank you for the watch.
I will treasure it with all of my heart.
Love you loads, Ashleigh-Mai.

Ashleigh-Mai Craig (11)
Highfields School, Penn

Victim

Bruises on my arms,
Scratches on my face,
Cuts on my legs
And what was the case?

All I did was spill my drink
And now I'm coughing blood in the sink,
Not even allowed to think,
It's like not even being able to fall on an ice rink.

He slaps me, punches me, spits on my face
And honestly, what was the case?

Who should I tell? Who can help?
Should I scream? Should I yelp?
Please, please call for help.

Santana Aspinall (13)
Highfields School, Penn

Global Warming

G lobal warming will affect all of us
L ess emissions
O ceans are rising
B ees are going extinct
A rctic is melting
L ots of wildfires

W eather patterns are changing
A ction, we need to act now
R ainforests are being chopped down
M ining - there is too much mining happening
I ce is melting
N orth Pole disappearing
G laciers melting.

Nihal Khular (14)
Highfields School, Penn

Mental Health

M e, you and everyone can experience it
E veryone can help you
N o one is left alone
T ogether we can help
A ll of us have it
L earn about it to help others

H elp others who suffer
E veryone deserves help
A lot of people have bad mental health
L ove yourself
T reat people with kindness
H eal the broken.

Arabella Watson-Wood (14)
Highfields School, Penn

Earthquakes

E cological damnation
A bysmal destruction from left and right
R umbling from down below
T he ground splintering
H azards everywhere
Q ueen of the ground erupting
U nderground tragedy
A nger from the stone
K iller splinters from the deep dark
E normous loss of innocence
S alute to the lost souls.

Edward Elrington (14)
Highfields School, Penn

Overcoming Bullying

It starts with one word,
One hateful word.
You feel destroyed but you let it go,
Maybe they won't do it again?

But then your peace gets shattered again,
Another hateful word gets blurted out.
They won't do it again, will they?

From what was once an infrequent comment,
Turns more frequent by the day,
Why would they do this to me?

Lydia Bray (14)
Highfields School, Penn

Penguins

Penguins squeak
but the numbers are weak.
They enjoy the sleet.
Soon they'll fade

and be forced to wade.
They won't last another decade.
Are you just going to sit there and drink Lucozade?
Your life won't be replayed.

Penguins have a nice beak,
They also reek
of fish, not beef.

Save the penguins.

Ryan Wentworth (12)
Highfields School, Penn

Online Harm And A Statutory Duty Of Care

You stole everything from me!
Yet you walk away with no fee.
How dare you.
Those days I sat on my own with no clue,
What on Earth did I do to you?
I tried to hide
But the hatred was too wide.
Sometimes I sit there
While you are unaware
The harm you cause me,
Yet you walk away with no fee!

Kenzie Cooper (13)
Highfields School, Penn

Kick It Out

K icking a ball
I sn't just football, it's a
C ommunity of fans and teams
K ick it out of football

I diots make racist comments
T owards players and staff

O nline or in matches
U nderline the issues
T o kick it out.

Solomon Diaram (13)
Highfields School, Penn

Ruined

Do you still laugh at those jokes?
Those jokes which ruined her pearly smile.
Those jokes which ruined her beautiful laugh.
Those jokes which ruined her joyful radiance.
Those jokes ruined her.
You ruined her.
And now, even when she's gone,
You can't admit you started the ruin of her.

Simar Badesha (14)
Highfields School, Penn

Climate Change

From fires to dried rivers
And polar bears with no shivers.
Rising temperatures go higher each year,
Animals have to live through death and fear.

Polar bears are under threat,
Governments, parliaments and ministers had targets to set,
But it looks like none of them will be met.

Areeg Elhassan
Highfields School, Penn

Neglected And Unwanted

I was left,
I was unwanted,
Not needed,
I was left to die.
I was sad,
Unhappy, unwanted,
But then you came along.
Now I'm happy and full of life,
What would I have done?
Probably shrivelled up and died,
If you never came into my life.

Zara Gittoes (14)
Highfields School, Penn

Racism In Football

R espect is key
A bysmal abuse
C ontrol your actions
I nconsiderate words
S peak with caution
M ind your words!

Oliver Simpson (14)
Highfields School, Penn

Wolverhampton Wanderers FC

W olverhampton Wanderers
O range strips
L embikisa
Ne **V** es
J **E** ff Shi
S teve Bull.

Phearan Hall (11)
Highfields School, Penn

The Earth Is Dying

The Earth is on fire so come and help me,
It's burning in the deserts and flaming in the trees.
The flames are rising high and the heat is killing me!

The Earth is getting colder, so come and help me,
It's snowing in California and raining in Italy,
The wind is getting colder and the cold is killing me!

The Earth is going extinct so come and help me,
It's losing all the animals and the turtles of the sea,
The pandas are dying down and the loss is killing me!

The Earth is becoming polluted so come and help me,
It's filled with plastic bottles and bags surrounded by creatures of the sea,
The air is filled with smoke and the clouds are filled with ashes and the fumes are killing me!

The Earth is dying so come and help me,
Its climate is collapsing and so is the sea.
The trees are being felled and collected for oil and the carbon's killing me!

The Earth is dying so come and help me!

Lottie Gormley (12)
Sibford Senior School, Sibford Ferris

Love

I hate you, I hate you, I hate you
But I can't
Because I love you
You make my heart ache every time I see your eyes
Every time I hear your voice
Every time I see you smile
It reminds me
It reminds me of when those starlit eyes used to look at me
When that gorgeous smile was aimed at me
When your soothing voice said the words, I loathe so much now
The words I love you
Now I know love is a lie
Love is fiction
Love was never there
Love is a word that blurs reality and blinds you from its true form
Love is a state of mind that is used in bad more than good
It's a weapon that stabs you in the back when you least expect it
Jealousy
Jealousy is love's best friend
It suffocates you and takes what it wants
It becomes you
It thrives when you say those dreaded words
It eats you from the inside out

It grows horns and a tail that scares away happiness
I hate it
So, I block out love in fear of it all happening again
But I can't stop thinking about it
About how you make me feel
I feel full around you, but I despise that
I base all my happiness on you, and it kills now you're not here
You're my sun on a cloudy day
My light in the dark
My rock to lean on
My shoulder to cry on
Now it's all gone
I see you happy, laughing, smiling, living, enjoying yourself
How do you do it?
How do you look at me and feel nothing?

How do you talk to me and put all our past behind you like it was never there?
How do you sleep at night without me saying goodnight?
How do you go out and look at other girls and not think about me?
Acceptance
We haven't talked for months now
You feel like a stranger
I look at your new girl and wonder what does she have that I didn't?
Is it her looks?

Is it the way she dresses?
Or the way she can say the words that have been stuck in my throat since the day we met
The words I love you...

Evie Bothwell (14)

Sibford Senior School, Sibford Ferris

Sorry

Dear future generations, I speak for everyone when I say sorry
Sorry for killing the orangutans, the tigers, the leopards
Sorry for killing the whales, the rhinos, the pandas
Sorry for killing the Earth
The waters are rising, towns are flooding
We hope you can forgive us, we didn't realise how special the Earth was
How beautiful she really is
We were wrong, we didn't know what we had until it was gone
The Earth is dying, we denied it until we realised
It was too late, we tried we really did, but the heat is getting hotter, the water is rising, icebergs are melting, we're sinking fast, all hope is lost...
Unless we work together, power through, kill the pollution, not the Earth, build solar panels, save the animals,
We can't go back but we can go forward, help make a change.

Emily Holdsworth (12)
Sibford Senior School, Sibford Ferris

My Mum

This life was never for me.
I've got a family back at home, just like the foe,
people like me on the other side of the street,
they are no different from we.
They have trenches and trees, shell shock and gunshots,
friends that fell and are angry at the foe
and still a life back at home with a family of their own.

Propaganda posted on every street,
with letters not truthfully told,
my words blocked out for weeks,
with no certain place of home, home comforts far from few,
only just one picture of you,
my belongings packed in a sack
that spends most of the time on my back,
with my heavy boots weighing me down,
feet soaked up from the ground,
with no light ahead, no tunnel of hope,
our men trudge through just like the foe.

My neighbour fell to his knees
begging for his life to be saved but he never saw the day,
the day when this would all be over
when the flags would wave high above every head
as we stand there proudly listening to what has been said,
the day when it is normal again,

where scares are few and friendships are made
with old and new just like the foe would have to.

Me and my foe nothing would have ever changed,
we were just neighbours over the way,
with stories to tell our families back home,
people we lost and friends we found,
we are both just the same,
the only difference is we live half a block away.

I love you Mum, stay strong.
I'll always come home and see you again soon.
Your dearest son.

Nancy Oldroyd (15)
Sibford Senior School, Sibford Ferris

Balance...

The pendulum swings all the way to the left.

The thylacine as beautiful as a polished ruby,
as effective a predator as a scimitar through hot scones,
its existence felled by fearful farmers.

The golden toad as elegant as a wounded deer,
yet as enthralling as the great works of Tolkien,
its existence put to an end by unwitting merchants bearing
a virulent but lethal fungus.

The dodo as harmless as a well-trained dog,
but as mystifying as a pilot-less plane,
its peaceful lifestyle devoured by gluttonous nautical
marauders.

The pendulum swings to the left, but not all the way yet.

The orangutan as inventive as any,
'Man of the forest' and with intelligence only surpassed by
us,
they have been put on the brink of annihilation by greedy
businessmen.

The Chinese alligator, a truly muddy dragon of the rural
lakes,
as legendary as its title,
its existence caused to wane because of the actions of
ignorant polluters.

The tree kangaroo as bizarre as a car without wheels,
but in the trees as elegant as a swan on water.
Being driven to the verge of destruction by excessive greed!

Thomas Heald (12)
Sibford Senior School, Sibford Ferris

The Bee

A bee went flying through the town,
it came to a standstill and fluttered down,
it landed on some bright red flowers,
the first it had found in many hours.

The town was now overpopulated,
growing flowers had become outdated,
the bee continued its weary search,
not passing over a single birch.

This bee was key to pollination,
a vital part in plant creation,
yet there was not a meadow in sight,
as it carried on its flight.

An urban landscape stood ahead,
the rising smoke would make the bee dead,
the humans used pesticides, which ruin beehives
and damage the health of the colony hives.

Invasive species roam the land,
arriving here from foreign sands,
the bee returned to the rows of hives,
these bees are slaves but no one cries.

It is time for the bees to be gassed,
in an unnatural place where they are all amassed
because of their precious honey
and our greed and want for money.

Alfie Jennings (12)
Sibford Senior School, Sibford Ferris

Fight For The Future

My future is a mythical creature
Lurking in the deep unknown
Twisted spine, crippled by poverty
Raging red eyes, engulfed in war
Ragged claws piercing icebergs
Breaking, falling, melting

My future walks on the dusty wheel of time
Searching for a spark of brightness
A forever flame of hope
With ambition in his pocket
Scattering scarlet trails of courage
Breathing, growing, glowing

My future is a second away
Often a year away
Sometimes a decade away, but always by my side
More than a friend
A partner in the whirlpool of life
Running, protecting, saving.

Thomas Jakeman (11)
Sibford Senior School, Sibford Ferris

If We Never Met

Imagine if we never met
I would be living my life in a meaningless way
The type of day you feel empty inside
Because there was nothing to feel
And you'd go back to how it was before we met
Which in my head I wonder would you wish that
But in reality, I know you'd feel the same
And thinking this way helps me realise
That I am so thankful to have you
And you have helped me so much
And helped me feel a little less sad
And a lot more confident about myself
I am no longer scared of what's to come
Because I know I feel safe
Knowing I'll be with you.

Erin Ellis (13)
Sibford Senior School, Sibford Ferris

Young Writers Information

We hope you have enjoyed reading this book – and that you will continue to in the coming years.

If you're the parent or family member of an enthusiastic poet or story writer, do visit our website **www.youngwriters.co.uk/subscribe** and sign up to receive news, competitions, writing challenges and tips, activities and much, much more! There's lots to keep budding writers motivated!

If you would like to order further copies of this book, or any of our other titles, then please give us a call or order via your online account.

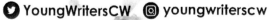

Young Writers
Remus House
Coltsfoot Drive
Peterborough
PE2 9BF
(01733) 890066
info@youngwriters.co.uk

Join in the conversation!
Tips, news, giveaways and much more!